'the'

charna ainsworth

August Publishing

ISBN: 978-1-7331452-3-7

Dedication

This collection of poetry is dedicated to you.
The you found in these words.

Contents

Complete...1

Enough...2

All Eternity...3

Pushed...4

Prying Eyes...5

Could Have..6

Tunnel Vision...7

Chasing the Light...8

Shut..9

Cleansed...10

Calm...11

Never Say Goodbye..12

No One... That's Who...13

Directions...14

Searching for Forever..15

All Your Weight..16

Results..17

Searching for Change...18

Out of My Control..19

Beginnings...20

'the'

Faithless...21

Speak..22

Dying Wish..23

Capturing Moments......................................26

Prediction...27

Breathtaking..28

If I Follow...29

The Hills..30

Façade..31

You...32

Dreamer...33

Soul's Core..34

Daisy..35

Possibilities...36

Emerald Coast...37

What Is Wrong...38

You and I..39

Poet's Heart...40

A Moment...41

Attempted...42

Choiceless...43

That Was Yesterday.......................................44

Wanting a Friend..45

What Didn't Kill Me...46

the depths..47

While You Are Here..48

Complete

When time collides
within the wall of prayers
the door will open up;
I'll be standing there,
and it'll be me...
that holds '*the*' key
to begin the rest of my life.
It won't be filled
with your tone
saying everything about me
is wrong,
your eyes will never
look at me
the way they do now.
I'll feel complete
for the first time,
without your judgment
upon me.
Yes, after I turn '*the*' key
I'll be free...
     ...forever.

Enough

Within the shield
behind the guard
placed over my heart
a girl who's alive
one not frightened to try
hides silently inside
waiting for her time
to speak the truth
traveling the world
just to protect little girls
from the brutal men
in this unjust world.

All Eternity

The space invaded
by your words
nothing but lies
is shaped by your hatred
darkened by your goodbye
seeking shelter
turned away
for lack of pride
I wanted
I needed,
given my all -
filled by your lies -
fallen into mediocrity -
rendered blind;

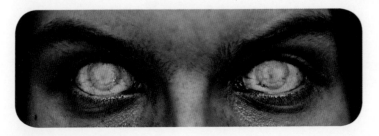

nothing really matters
this life will soon be over;

your crimes will live on forever.

Pushed

taken with hope
you might just care
show me kindness
just be there
when I'm needing
a shoulder
a friend

how I wish
it were true,
now I know
about you,
the sadness
of your face
looking down on me
with pity
with distaste…

cruel to say the least
sad to know
the truth;
you're a liar
and a thief,
I no longer
want anything
to do with
someone like you.

Prying Eyes

she was the last of her kind
drifting slowly out to sea
nothing behind
could stop her
the vision was clearly
beyond the reach
of the place
she once called home,
empty and barren
she left all alone
in search of a life
to call her own
without any judgment
of evil
or prying eyes
to witness mistakes
and little white lies,
they all turned to grey
when she walked away
from the life she knew before,
it was easy to say goodbye,
only one tear
left her beautiful eyes
as the boat left the shore...
never to return.

Could Have

He was wrong about me
his words were all lies
sad to say it took many years from me
to understand why he felt the need
to keep me down,
what sadness to think of what might have been

if he'd held me up... cherished my love,
brought out the best in me
instead of feeling like
he'd been given my love
only to break me down
to make him feel high
to squash my dreams...
instead of watching me fly.

Tunnel Vision

There are things I said
lingering in your heart
words to empower
giving life when remembered.
It was simple then
to believe the impossible,
definition of dreamer -
not knowing the obstacles
that soon liter the path
too many obligations>
look at the fingers in the pie,
why should we strive another
moment

letting go, we could release the lie
that bargains with souls
stealing their dreams
until they find themselves old
and it's too late
for what might have been…
what could have been…
if they had never given up.

Chasing the Light

straggling the center
opposite the ends
of instruction
and correction
where fool's follow
chasing the light
that beckons…
it calls
promising more
than anyone could define:
keeps the man
lingering in the room;
women stay seated
afraid to appear eager
of a chance
life can be bigger
than food stamps
and HUD housing.
raging rivers
of goodness
drown simple men
while others
wade bravely
turning sorrow to gold
as water rushes by…

Shut

I can only imagine
the monumental complaints
of how I took up space,

wasted oxygen…
while sitting alone
in a tiny dark bedroom
at the end of a trailer.
How I tried so hard
to stay out of sight
to grow smaller with time,
to breathe less…
but of course,
it was no use
I couldn't do anything

right
so I kept my mouth
shut tight
dreaming of my future life
in silence.

Cleansed

Falling past a thousand chances
to not live another day
with your horrid hate;
hoping, wishing, praying
you'll find a way
to tame your demons,
forcing your mind to think straight,
leaving the past behind
with all its mistakes,
embracing the future…
even find love for today,
it could shatter
all the harsh words
and wash away the pain
before I'm certain
to run far, far away.

Calm

trouble
oh, my soul has tasted trouble
found it bitter
spat out the worst
took off running
perpetually in search of peace,
oh, sweet peace

that comes from quiet within
        …a soul
knowing it's worth
refusing to give in or give up
the serenity it's known
for days   -   for months
for weeks   -   for minutes,   or hours
when troUble let it be,
yes, in that time
feeling completely free… from care.

Never Say Goodbye

it was the only way to say goodbye
turn the hope into fear
running with vigor
leaving with might
erasing the memory of you
from every aspect of the life
dreamed about for eternity
to fill the days
accepting every single part
of what they call your soul
becoming too close
losing control
until where I began
and where you end
blurred beyond reason
no one else could comprehend
the depths
I would have gone
to never say goodbye
to the only person on earth
who made me truly feel alive

No One… That's Who

Failure to mature
To reach full potential
Living under the standard
Set before me
When I was little,
Blistering cold
The way the winds blows
Through an empty life
When you have
No one to hold
Accountable for what's been done
Or who could listen
To what's been said
In order for
Something as simple
And complex
As this person's life
To go unread
Is the saddest story
That's ever been written,
Now there…
Feel better…
It's been said.

Directions

Follow your heart wherever it may lead
it's within the darkest hour
the light...

you can plainly see.
When you must decide
between right and wrong,
let there be no hesitation
of what the answer should be.
I've given you skills
and enough love to fill an empty sea...
now go live your life
and remember
whatever is to be... will be.

Searching for Forever

Crystal eyes of love
staring at the ceiling
as arms cradle
souls unite,
why...
so far away
in your head
in your thoughts
searching for forgiveness
in order to give
your all.
Will it be found
in such large amount?
These ugly deeds
are mounting
up to goodbye.
Forgive?
Most certainly.
Live a lie?
Not on your life.

All Your Weight

Within the womb
of hatred and regret

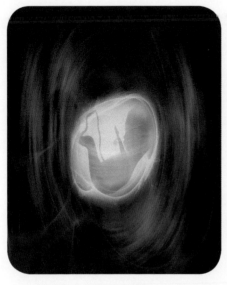

poisoned by cigarettes
and thoughts of
why
ruining your perfect life
before taking
a first breath
was a lot to lay
on a perfect soul
unblemished
by your truth
of never wanting
of never needing
me.

Results…

No more diving deep
memory serves
keeping altered hearts
in the shallows
where it hurts less
than it should.
The irony of it all
is the fear
that only exists
in the aftermath
of this terrible mess.

Searching for Change

blue highway
built on lies
covered in schemes
of making more than we ever seen
in our simple lives
of trailer park rules and childhood games

always searching for change
to escape the past where nothing could last;
it was all broken,
nothing smooth about it,
still we rode...
what else did we know but to ride it out,
bumpy or not,
it was a one-way... one way or another
we would burn that path right into a future
that didn't in any way resemble the tainted past

Out of My Control

My hunger speaks of a distant day
when love was ripped away
from the depths of a little girl's soul.
I was crying as I clung…   to the only one who would run
if I needed anything at all.

The tragedy struck deep
…to the point I would never speak,
with the same voice, ever again.

Beginnings

blood like water
wearing away imperfections
eroding all roughness
evading the soul
the heart of everything
given at birth
beautiful
no question
destined to persevere
reaching heights beyond imagination
without your hate
despite your crimes
no longer lying in wait
of the best;
simply walking away
from what's left of I love yous

Faithless

Words spoken over me
for harm
for good
etch so deeply
in my soul

bringing pain
bringing joy
building my faith
to crash again
at the mention
of your name.
Why do you speak
such mean things
over me?...
- when at this moment
I am
the one and only person
you have

in this world
who still believes
in you....

Speak

There…
pressed against the paper
in my mind's eye
I see the future
full of potential
ripe with rewards
for labor so deep
week after week
of pen and of paper
collecting the life
right out of my mind
fueling the next readers
with precious resource
uncommon to as many
who discovered their voice
    and use it.

Dying Wish

He was sitting comfortably,
when I spoke up and asked…
what is your dying wish?
A quiet voice that trembled and swayed
answered in the twilight…
at the end of day
I've never wanted much
all my life… you see
I was happy for the good ole' days,
sad to see them leave…
and there was magic
in the sadness
that's hard to describe
kinda like that feeling
when you're standing on the peak
of that mountain you just climbed,
but if I could ask for anything
before I pass on from this life
it would be one more day
with my children and wife.
One of the good ones
full of sunshine
when we were together,
our bodies full of laughter
our hearts full of love.
I moved a little closer
when I saw the twinkle in his eyes
he smiled as best he could

while I thought of a reply.
I'll go get them,
just tell me where they are
it doesn't matter how near
or how far,
I will find them
and I'll bring them to you;
it's your dying wish
it's the least I could do.
He cleared his throat,
the twinkle left his eyes
he stuttered at first
over the words in his mind.
I had two daughters and a son
and one beautiful wife
she passed away
about a decade ago;
I lose track of time.
My son went off to war
came home in a wooden box;
it broke my wife's will to live,
which in turn, broke my heart.
My firstborn daughter…
she's out in the world,
probably doing good.
It's been years since we spoke;
she always thought, I was no good
You see,
her husband's family
made a lot of money in oil

and her old father
never measured up.
My baby girl's been gone the longest,
we lost her when she was twelve.
It was a hit-and-run.
People always talked
like it was her fault,
said she shouldn't have been
riding her bike after dark.
So… you see young lady…
my wish,
it's impossible to fulfill
unless…
I fall asleep and dream
escaping back into the memory
of one perfect peaceful
spring day in May.

Capturing Moments

Talent can't be learned
only sharpened like a knife
against a smooth stone;
my stone is called life.
Once when I was little
I found a magic pen,
it loved white paper,
it became my cherished friend.
The letters did fall
in perfect array
speaking of the wisdom
to release me from the past.
So… I grew
as the words compiled into memories;
capturing moments,
preserving for all,
a glimpse of talent,
sharpened by time
and life's smooth stone
combined with a never-ending rhyme.

Prediction

you can't see
what I've been through
by looking at me,
it's been uphill
-both ways-
most of my life;
funny
what was meant to destroy
strengthen me beyond scope
of what the critics predicted
of what the haters said
but there is no one
to be proud
of where I am
rising above
where I come from
except me;
for the first time
that's enough.

Breathtaking

I am the author of my life.
I get to write the story.
Each word
I choose on purpose.

Every scene has a reason.
The story I tell is not perfect.
Sometimes, it's a rewrite.
Sometimes, just an edit...
but every once-in-a-while;
it's simply breathtaking.
I close my eyes
savoring it -
the moment
I wrote... only in my mind
now played,
fleshed out... called my life.

If I Follow

There's a force that's invisible
lifting me into the light
giving me purpose and meaning
showing me exactly what's right
for my life.
The path
I must take
in order to fulfill
the mission God gave -
and if I follow...
if I succeed...
you can lay me to rest,
and please...
don't forget
to remember me.

The Hills

Days pass
blurring reason
pursuing purpose
in the hours
in the days
I have yet to live
wanting to fulfill
to be beloved.
Humans are lost,
look at the eyes
that disapprove
and every time
I die a little more.
There is only one,
the one on high
who knows my heart,
His love
is enough,
His strength
is sufficient,
I'll keep
traveling on
until the day
I'm finally home.

Façade

Religion has failed
as miserably as
misery can be
to be an answer,
a final solution
of what's ailing me.
Their fake love
given as a gesture
to prove their love for You
is dry; it's cold
and it will never do.
Anything to heal
the scars that just won't heal…
their fakeness can't reach
into my real.
Now that I think of it,
it's the epitome of oil and water.

You

Wonder
beyond all measure
Proof
love still exists
Reason
to not merely drift
through these days
called life.
When the purpose waivers
and the pollution comes in
your smile
fills me up
keeps me afloat
just enough
to carry on
giving strength to hold

this pen
and capture the moment
no longer held within
a heart too guarded
to share the truth;
That's you.

Dreamer

There is no way I'm giving up
no, I'm not backing down
I've been on this ride before
I'm no stranger to this town
see, I've been searching
all my life
for a dream that's going to come true
and nothing and no one
is going to stop me;
I'll never quit until
I break-through
and my reality
becomes the vision
I hold in my mind,
no more holding back
I'll keep on grinding
until I possess
this dream of mine.

Soul's Core

When the storyteller
fails to deliver
a juicy tale
full of love and hate
what will be his fate?...

in a world
driven by the lust
of more and more and more.
Will he be loved
for all the words written,
all the poems freely
given?
Can anyone appreciate
the continual saCrifice

displayed upon the page
as his soul gave and gave?
When his world is at an end
will you read his words once again

finding new meaning, wisdom and truth?
He gave them all to you
without remorse or regret
revealing his soul's core
until the very end.

Daisy

Pretty girl
all in white

you looked at me
and I knew
we were meant to be

still, you looked so sad…
the unchosen
in a crowded room

no one wanted you

but I could see
past your scars and scabs

see who you could be
with love

a beautiful Daisy
to brighten our world.

#rescuedog

Possibilities

there was a whisper on the wind
leading me time and again
to your door,
it was there I found a friend
who understood where I'd been
and cared enough
to show me there's more,
with time I stood up
and bent to my knees
it was then my friend
helped me find me,
it became so clear
I was meant for so much more
than I ever thought possible
before I walked through his door
now every day is better
I was blessed by knowing this man
glad I listened to the whisper
because meeting him was part of the plan

Emerald Coast

Taste the salty sea
from your breath
wave hello to the sun
let toes dance
upon grains of quartz
give your body and soul
a chance to become one
with the shore
with the sand
with the water; so blue
in that moment
you'll understand
all this paradise
has to offer you.

What Is Wrong

If I live another day
I'll search for ways
to get things right
inside my head
inside my mind
where carousels and
rocket ships
go round and up
never crashing down;
no, I'd be high
above what is wrong
with music and laughter
and unbelievable faith
that would make me stronger
than any of the previous days
I've spent
marking off my to-do list…
if I live another day.

You and I

when time rushes by
in a perpetual race
of to-dos
and don'ts
just remember my face
the way we used to laugh
it was our personal song
our souls private dance
no one else was invited
how I miss those days
sometimes, I find myself
longing for times…
when you and I smiled
and shared a warm embrace

Poet's Heart

I will not be ignored
you will remember my name
my words will live on
many years after I'm gone
they will find my books
on a dusty shelf
read them out loud
discussing what they
think the words meant
to a girl like me
on the day I wrote them down
but their true meanings
will be forever hidden
buried with the girl
brave enough
to share her poet's heart
with the world.

A Moment

Wind blows gently
Owl sings his song
Thomas meows
Stretching out his arms
The chimes play a melody
A red cow eats grass
There's a voice in the distance
The dog stops to scratch
A poet searches for words
To write down
Hoping they will forever last
An alarm reminds her
Time is moving fast
Like a river
Not far from the front porch
All the water flows south
And the words; they flow
In every direction
To and fro
Until the end of life
As *the* poet knows it.

'the'

Attempted

Carried by your whim
into an angry night,
blindly trusting
you with my life.
A split-second decision,

jealousy driving you mad.
Packing what little we had
while begging not to go.
As daylight turned to darkness,
no forethought in your plan
…left us
stranded between mountains.
Strong winds
blew foreign snow
with passion and force.
The car stalls

in the darkness
of white out.
Unprepared teenagers
trying to escape death
give their last dollar
to a tow-truck driver.
Just an angel in disguise
one November night
on Laramie's pass.

Choiceless

Saving up the vile
for when we're alone
pouring it out
upon my soul
I'm weak
always weak
wanting it to work
still trapped
in the fairy tale lie
that God sent you
only, the God I know
would never send
someone like you...
unbalanced and rude,
stealing my truth
with hatred and lies
leaving me no other choice
than to say goodbye.

That Was Yesterday

Who is going to have my back
when it's all said and done?
It's too easy
for you to walk away,
forget that we shared love
forget the words you'd say…
yet I still remember
every single one.
Especially the words
when you're discouraged
reminding me of
what you once had
and how I've let you down
time and time again.
Still, the one thing I wonder,
which will soon be your regret;
is when did it become
my fault
you don't have a perfect life
with a silver platter under it?

Wanting a Friend

when the walls are set
tall and wide and strong
no one can climb over
no one can break through
unless I choose to let them in,
it's defense at its finest
a prayer and a wish
hoping to divert disaster
remembering the pain of before
on the days
when I left the door…

open
wanting a friend
needing someone to care
without a dagger in their hand
or a lie on their lips

What Didn't Kill Me

Whispers and stares
follow my back
as I walked cautiously
through the crowd
of people who know
I'm no longer their prey
or hidden away
from their eyes.
Now I'm wide open,
healed from the pain.
The words they threw
to make them feel big
only made me better…
      made me stronger
so I could live
a life to be proud of
where I no longer hide;
I'm completely me,
Yes, and finally happy.

the depths

Alone in a crowd
you sought me out
to fill the void
inside the depths
of your heart.
Now I wonder
what did you see
the first night
you laid eyes on me?
Within our embrace
I found my place
in the endless world
of relentless strangers.
By the rising sun
my life had become
a matter of finding
my way back to
your sweet embrace.

While You Are Here

Golden light
falling from heaven
embrace your path
ordained before time
watch the sky open wide
with one word,
      one thought
of goodness and happiness
suffer not at anger
it is useless
wasting precious energy
better spent
on laughter and forgiveness
it's the place
you are predestined to live
why you are here
such gifts to give
remember it's freeing
to love more than hate
and maybe the only way
your soul will feel safe
and sheltered from this place.

Beloved reader,

You are there; on the pages, in the words. *You…* and only *you,* is who *'the'* is dedicated to. When I was a little girl, I began searching for someone… anyone to read, and understand. With every poem, with each page, I drew closer and closer. Your hands hold moments of life: captured in prose. Your eyes give meaning to the words. Your heart was *the* key for me to open my heart. Thank you for taking this poetic journey. Know you are loved and appreciated more than words could ever say. I will forever be grateful to *you* for turning the pages and finding yourself in the beauty, in the ashes, and in the triumph of *'the'*.

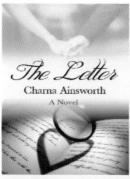 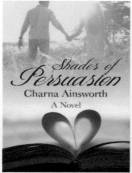 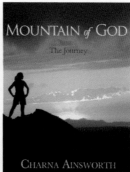

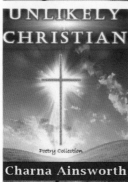 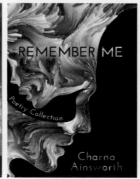 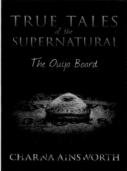

www.charnaainsworth.com

about the poet -

Charna Ainsworth is a novelist and an award-winning poet. She lives in South Mississippi, outside of a small southern town with her family.

What's coming next?

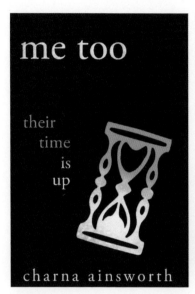

Reviews are welcomed and appreciated. Links to multiple book venues are located at:
www.charnaainsworth.com